Forme

Colorea libra

Coloring Pages for Kids

Coloring Pages for Kids
An imprint of Ciparum LLC

Forme colorea libra
© 2017 Ciparum LLC
All rights reserved.
ISBN-10:1-63589-413-1
ISBN-13:978-1-63589-413-4

Coloring Pages for Kids

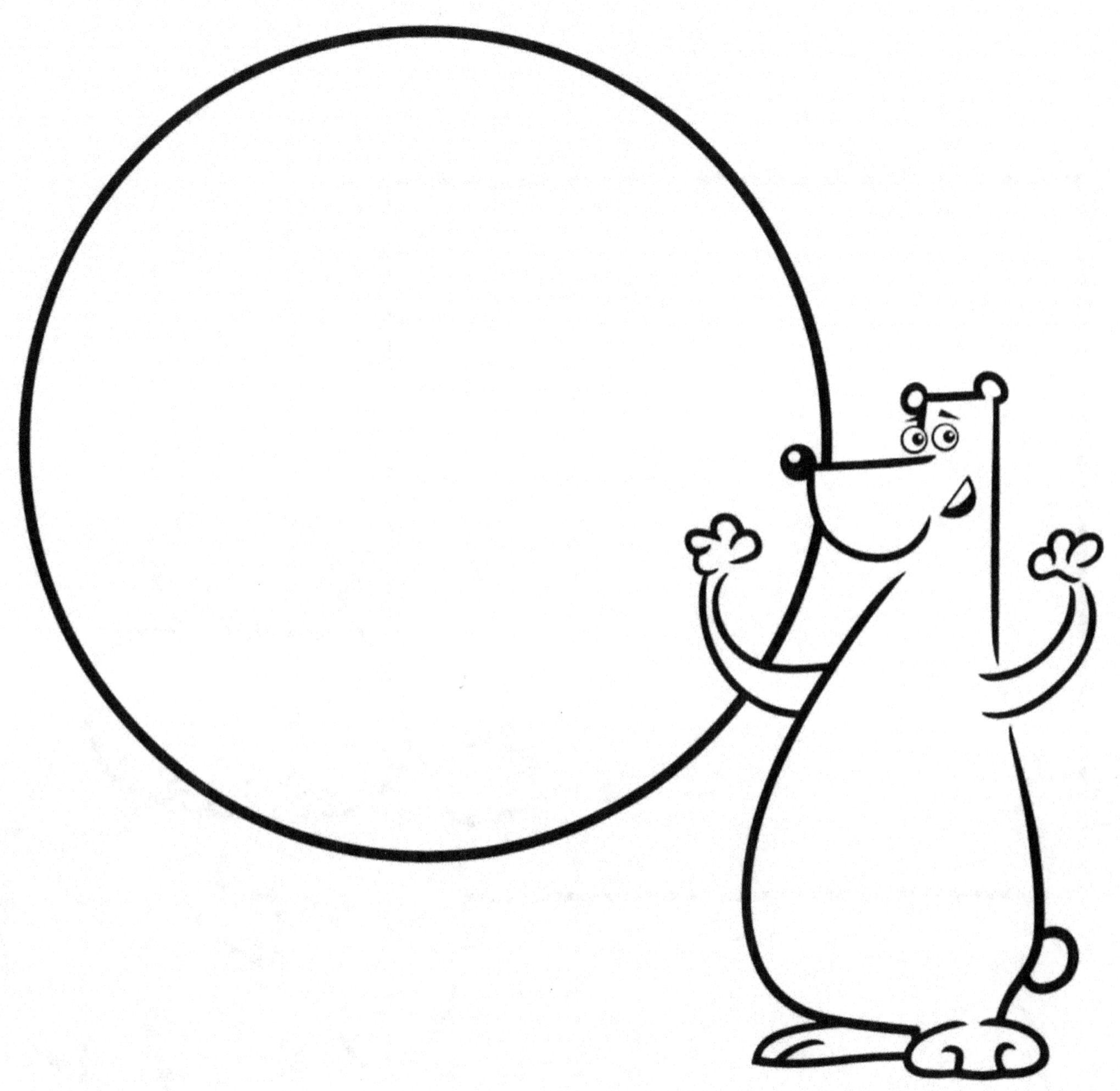

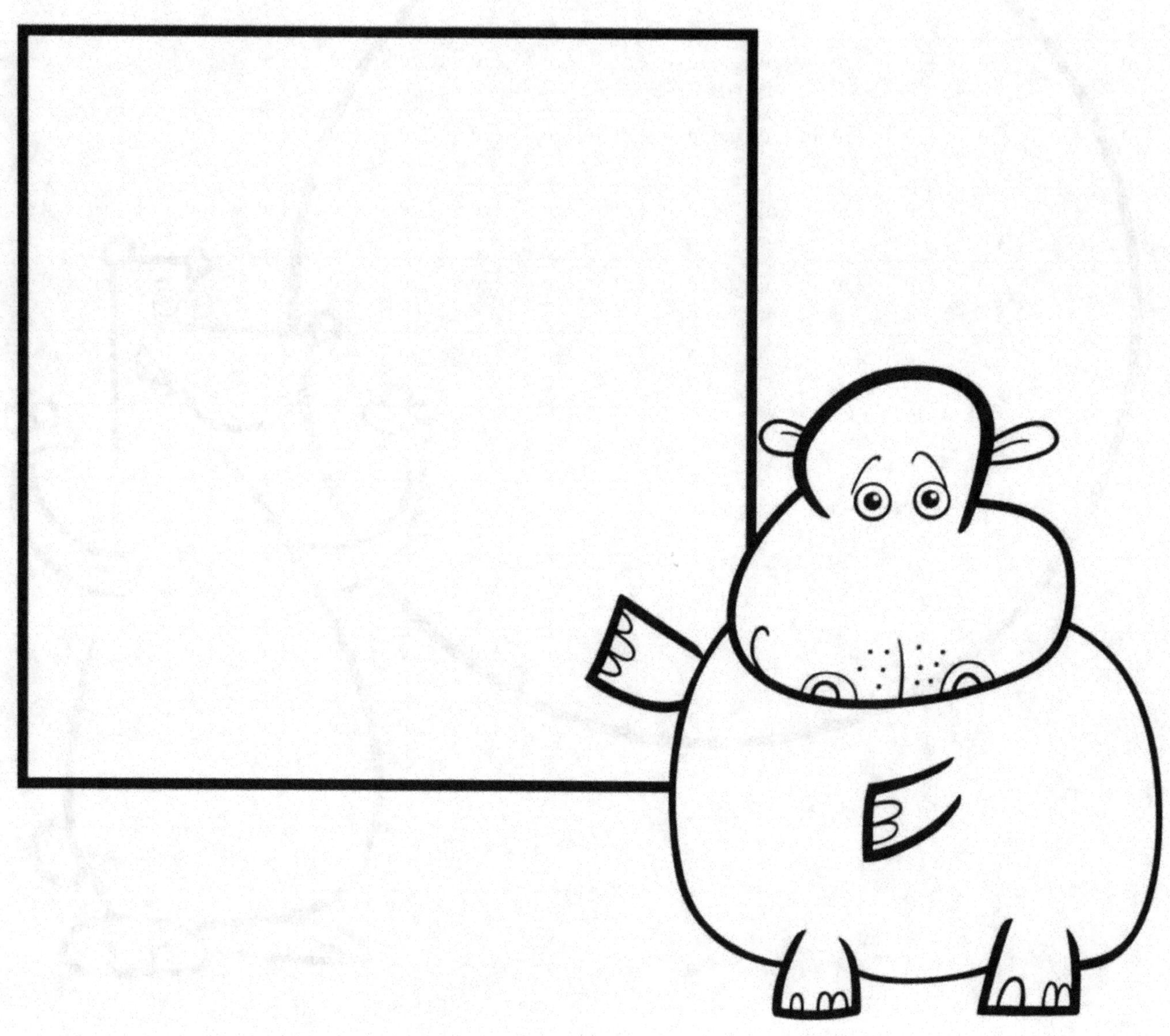

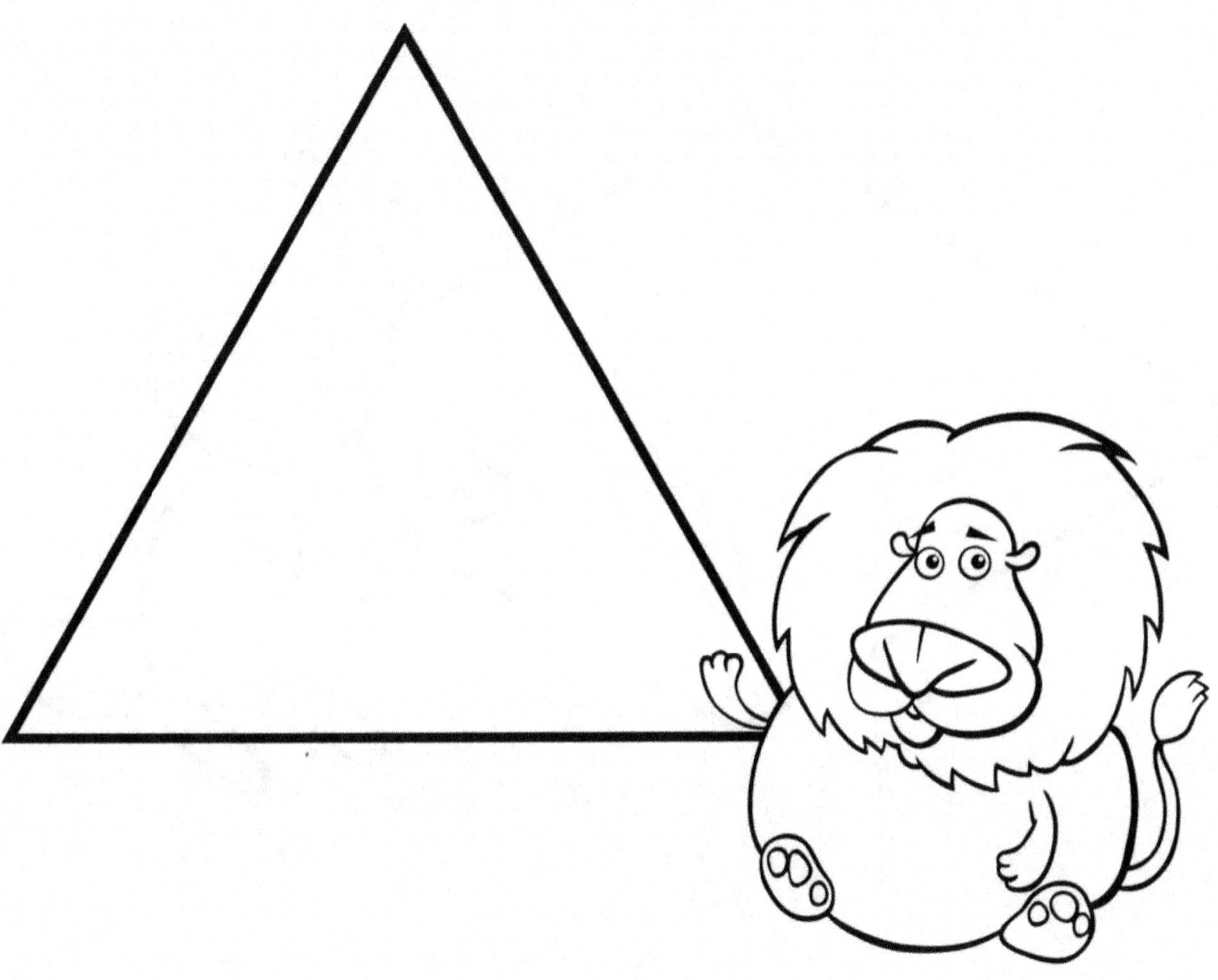

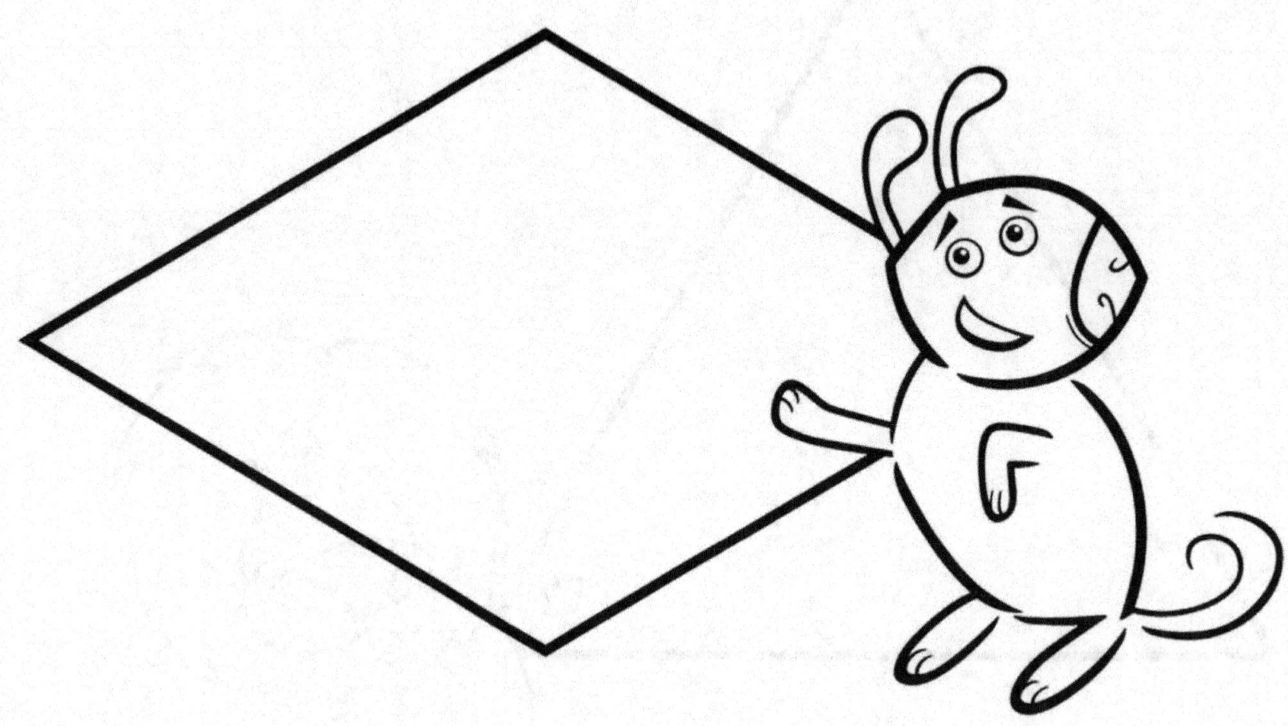

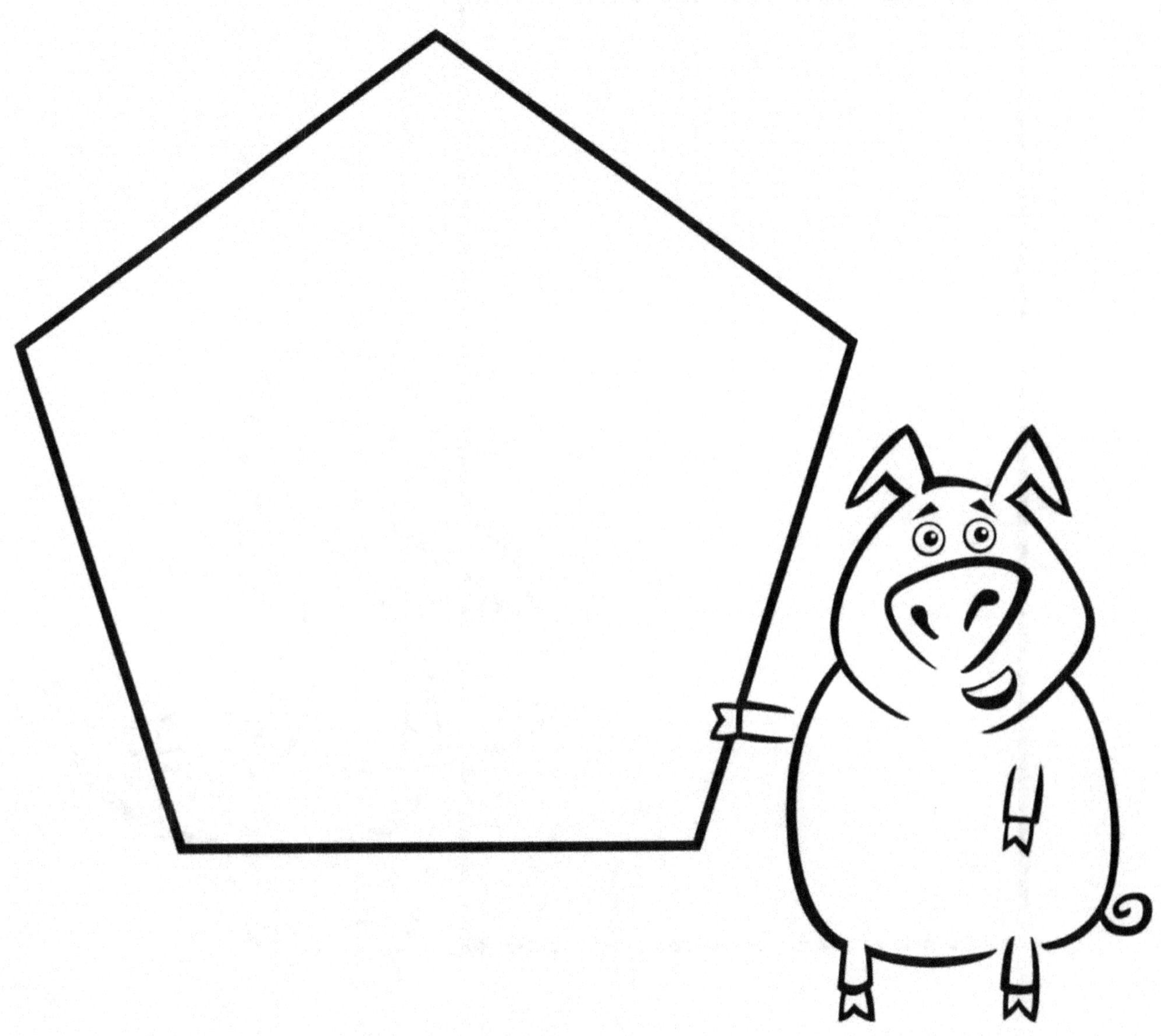

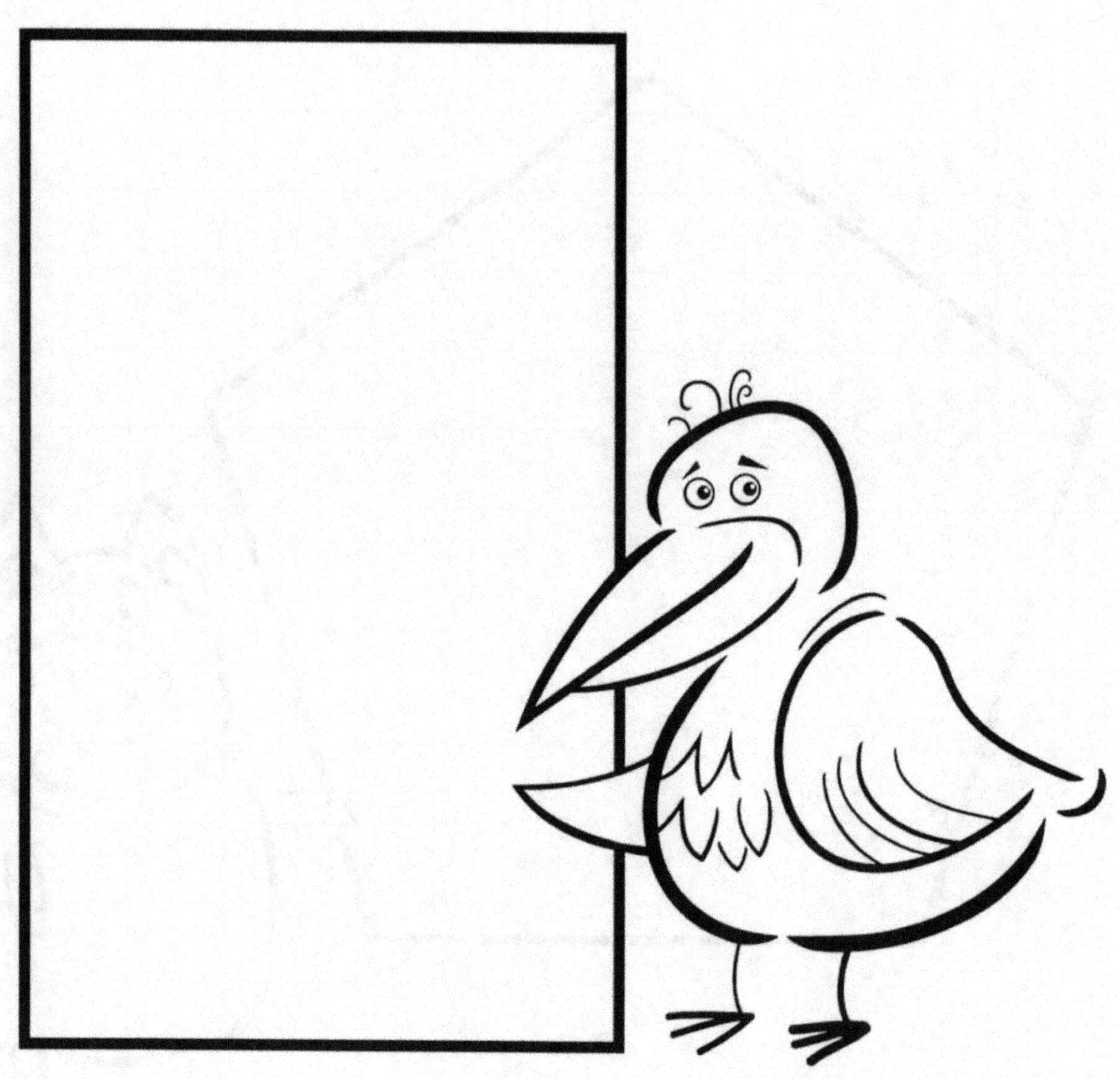

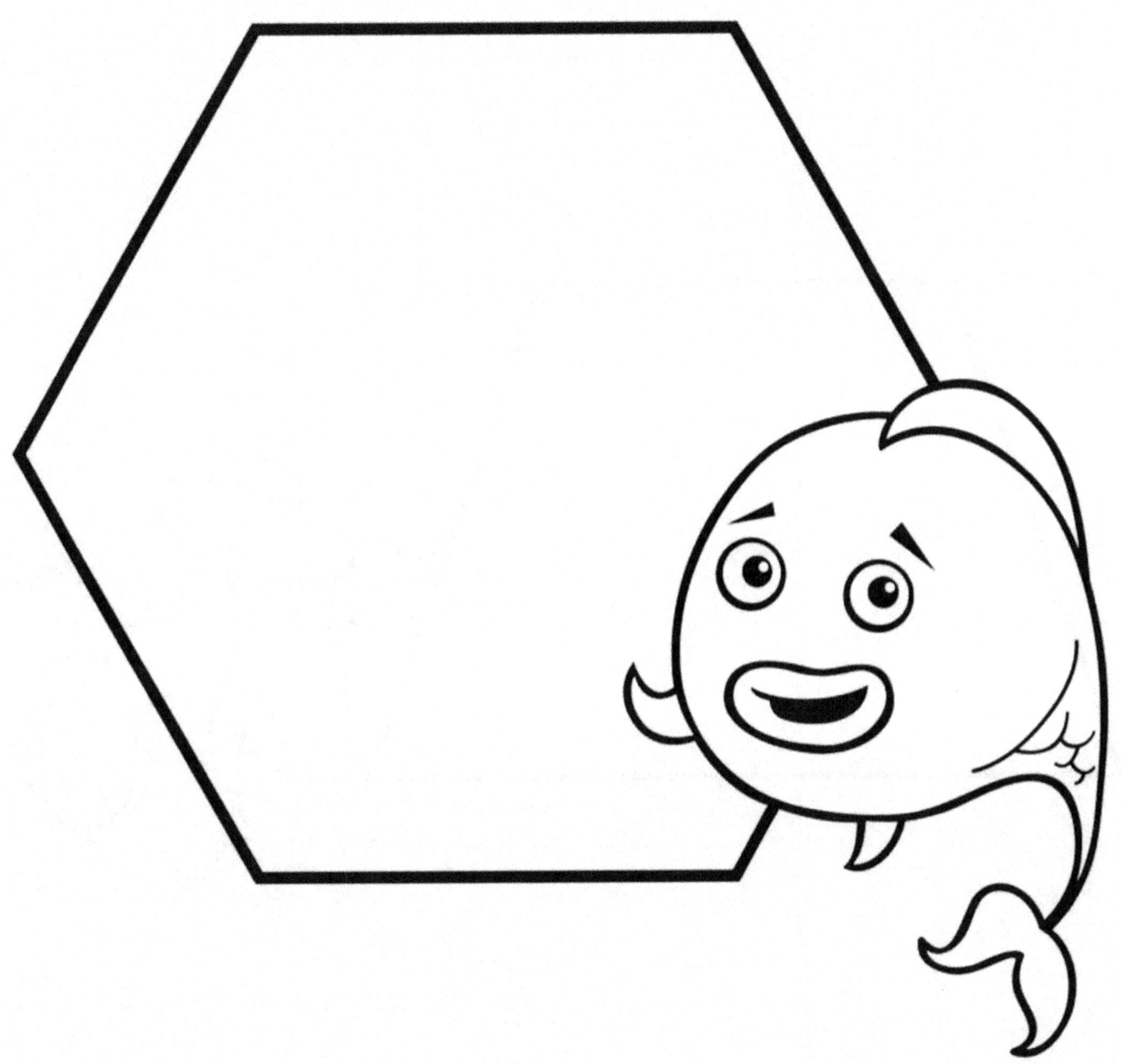

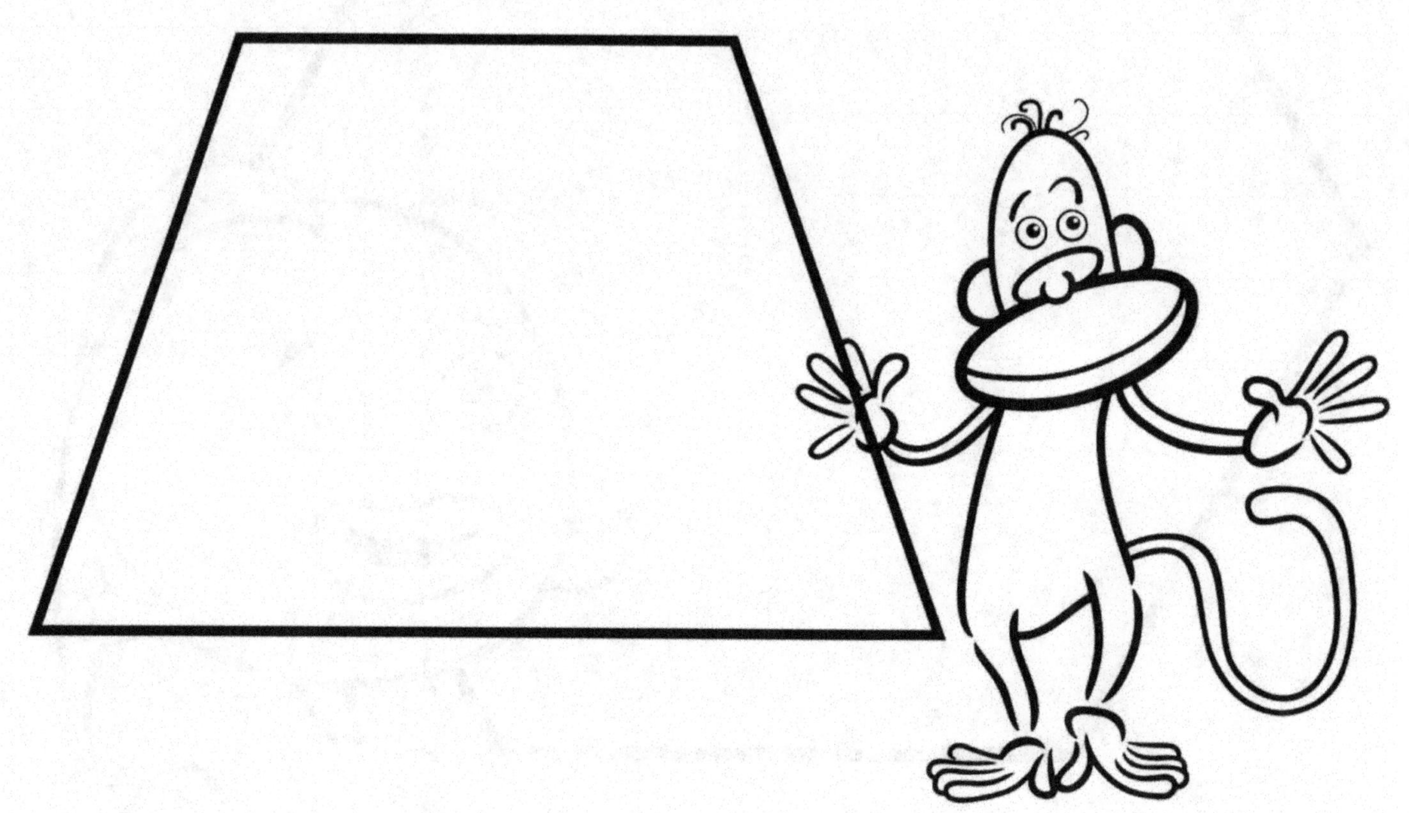

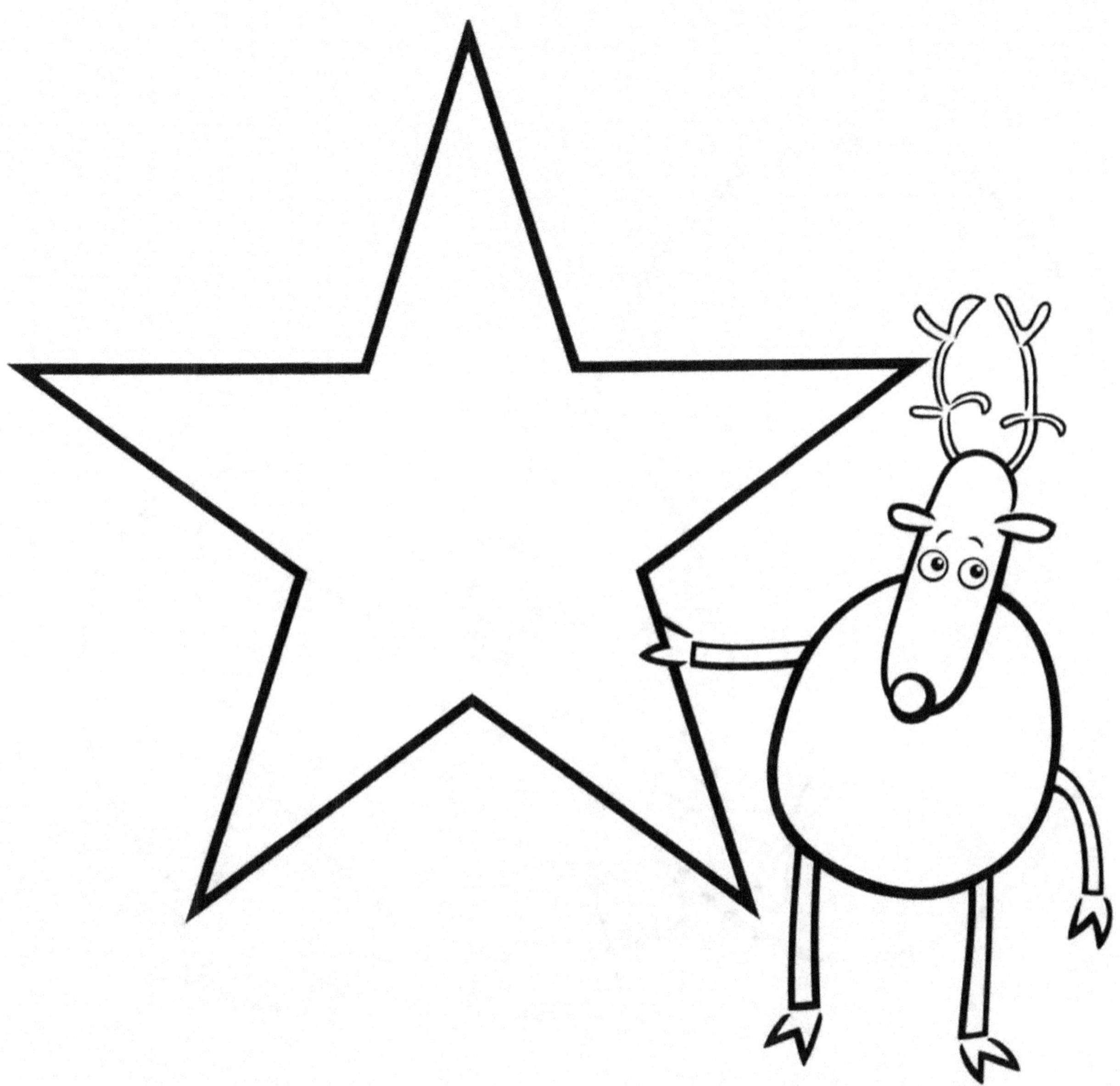

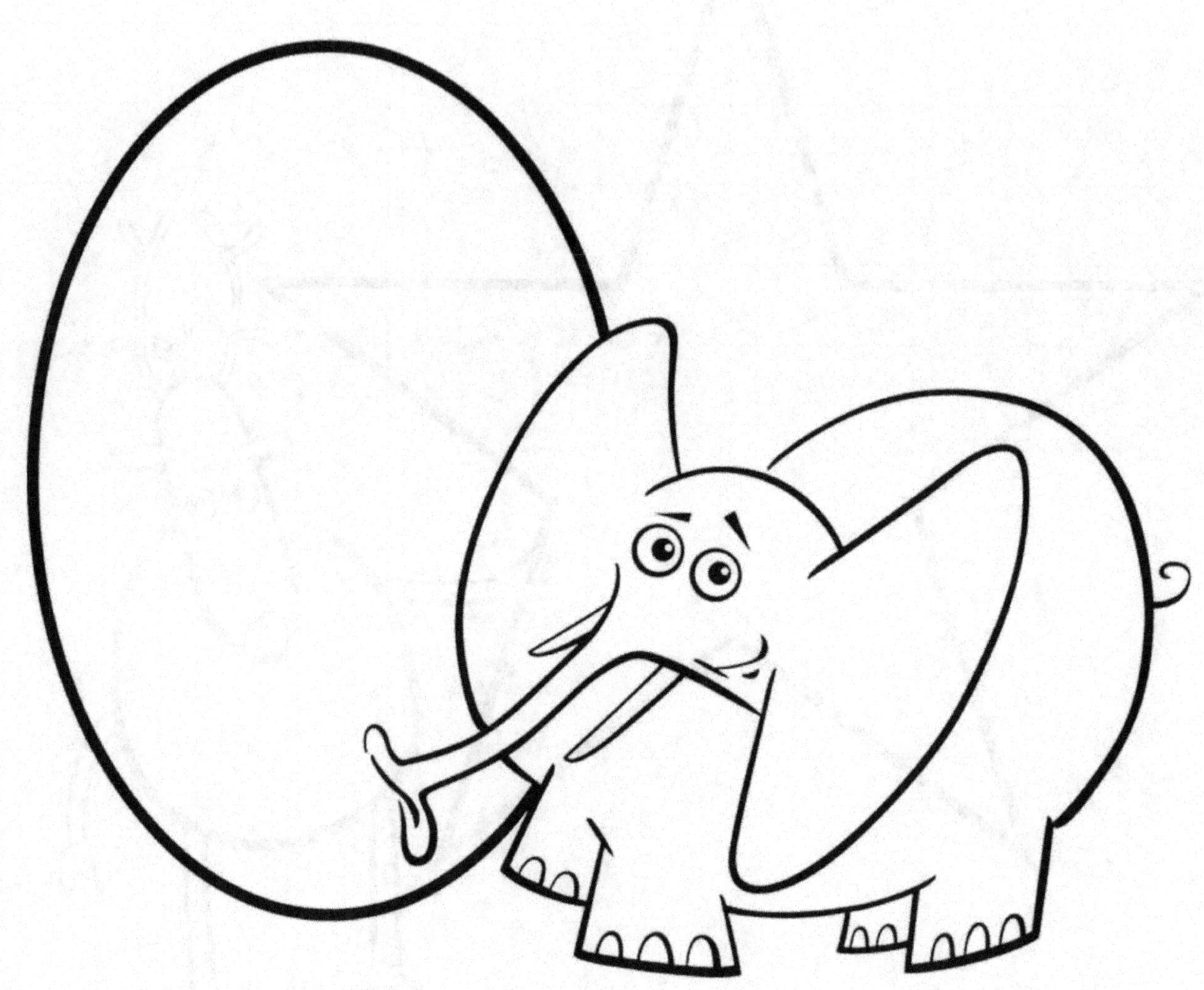

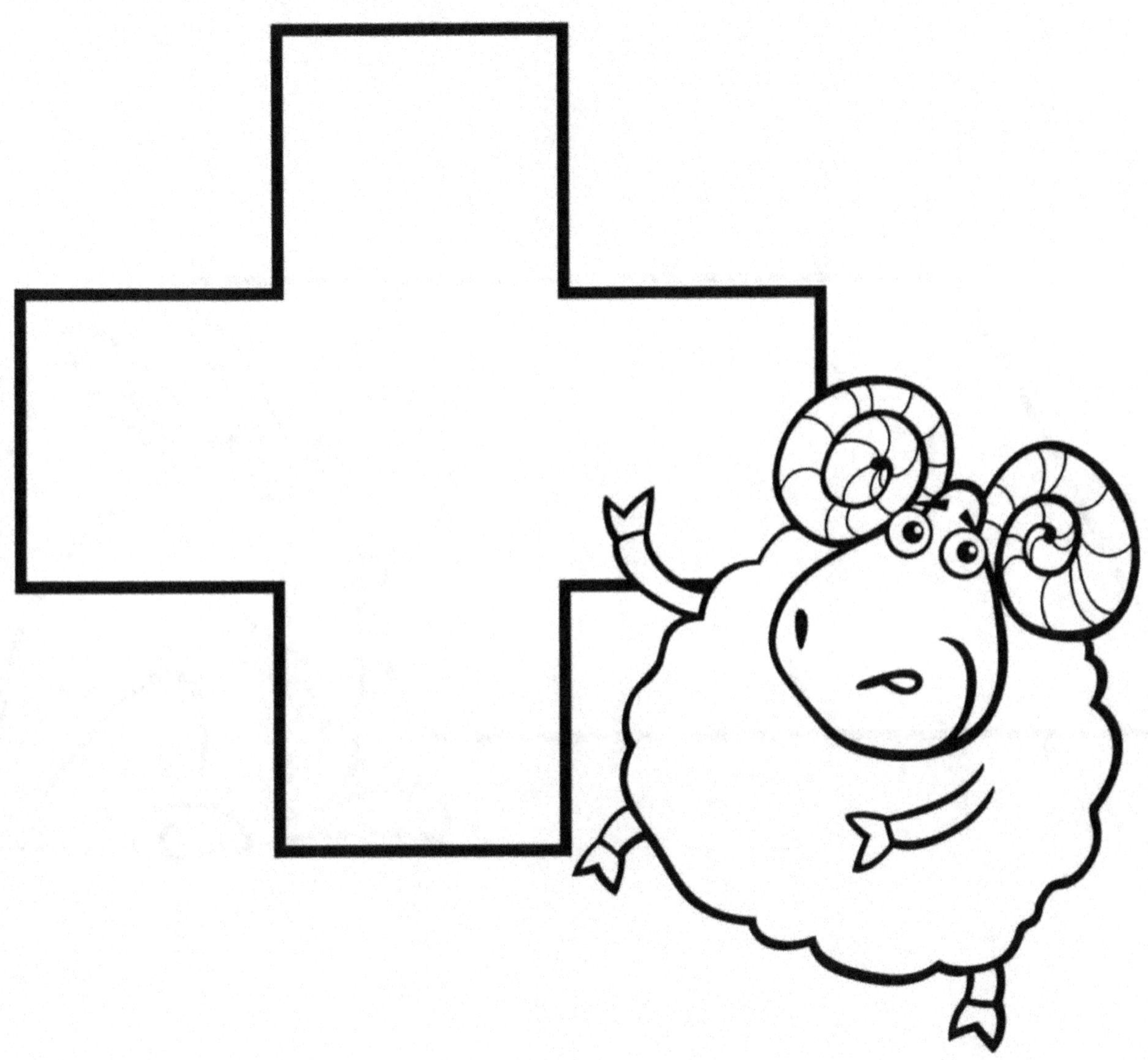

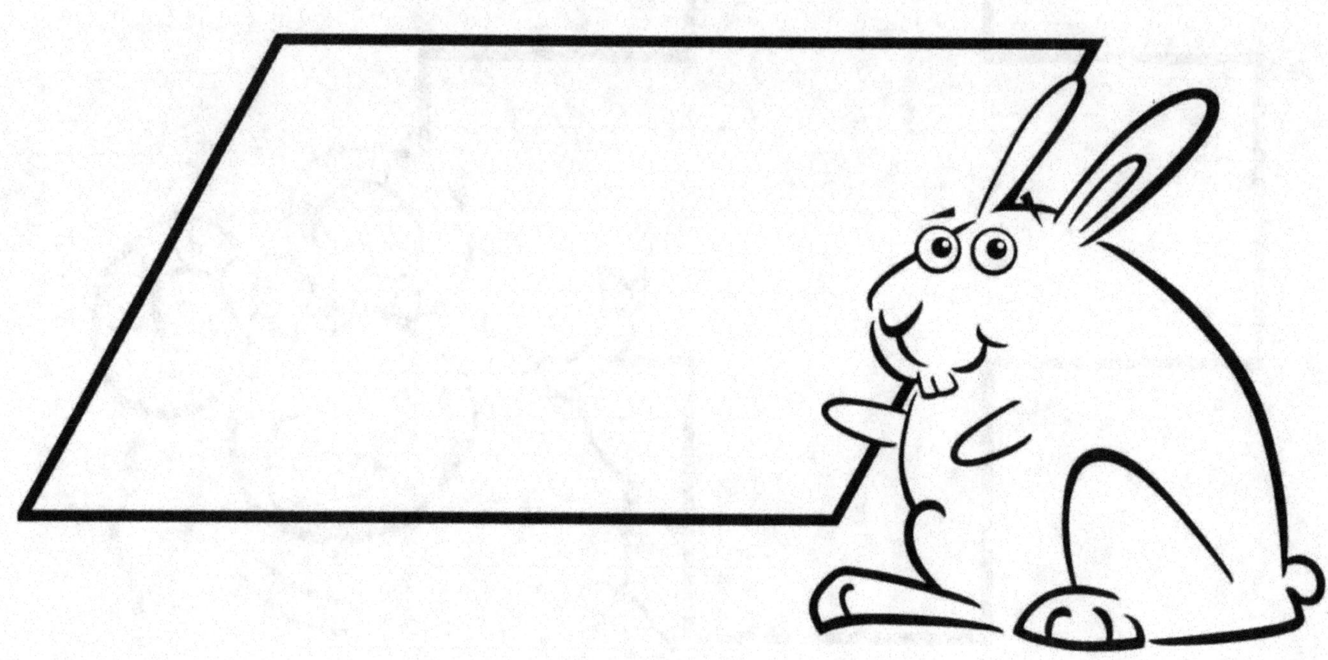

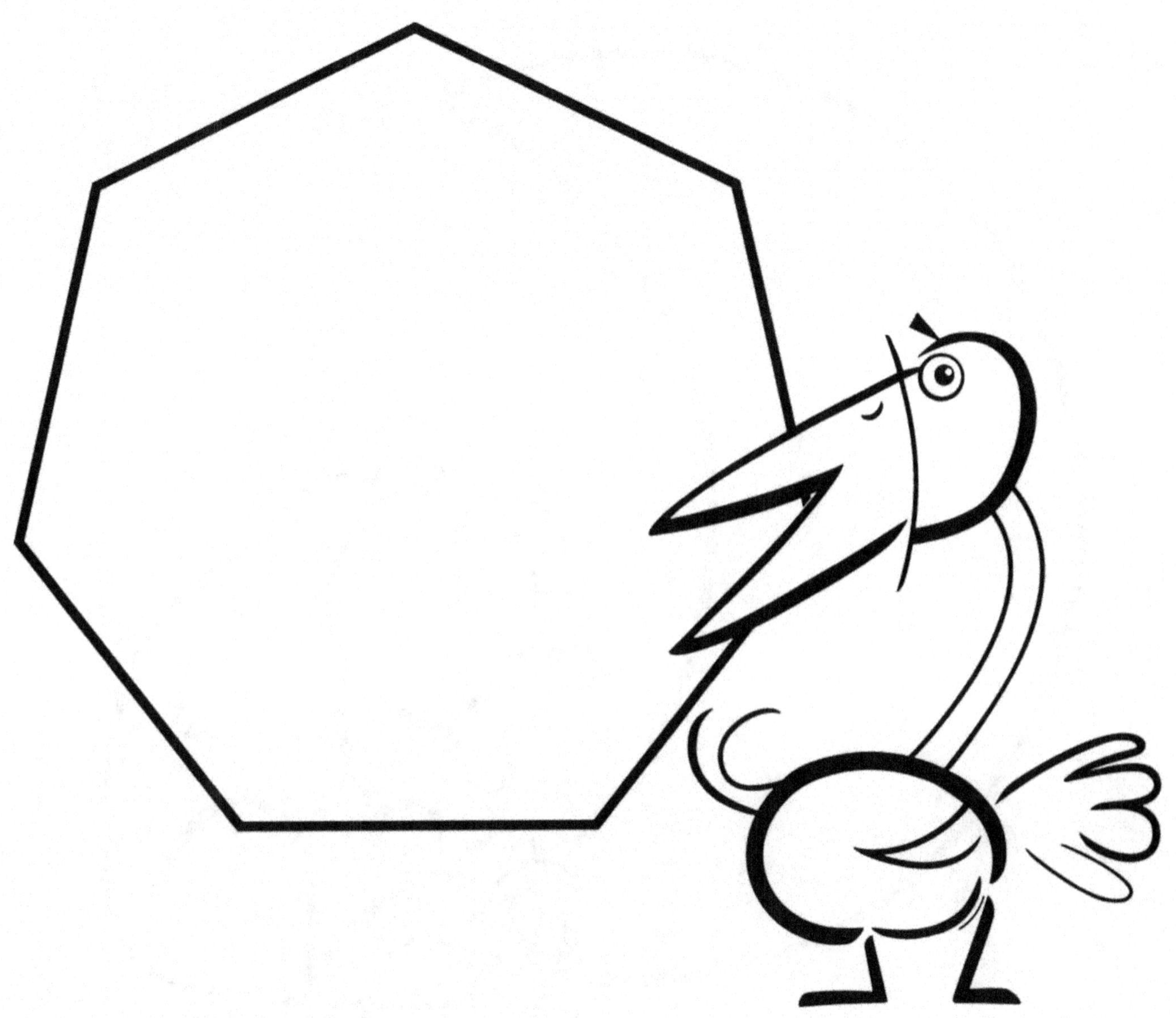

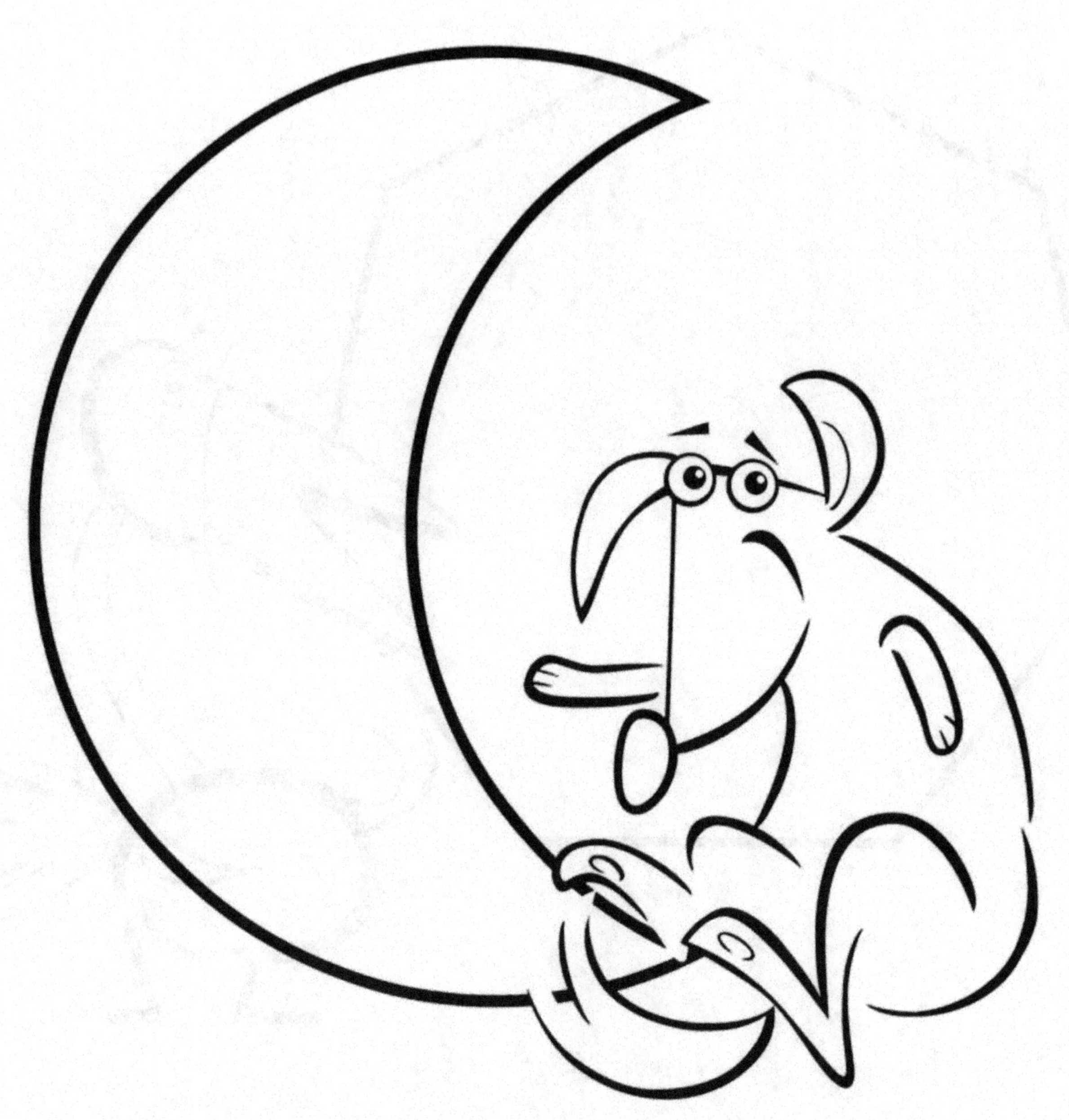

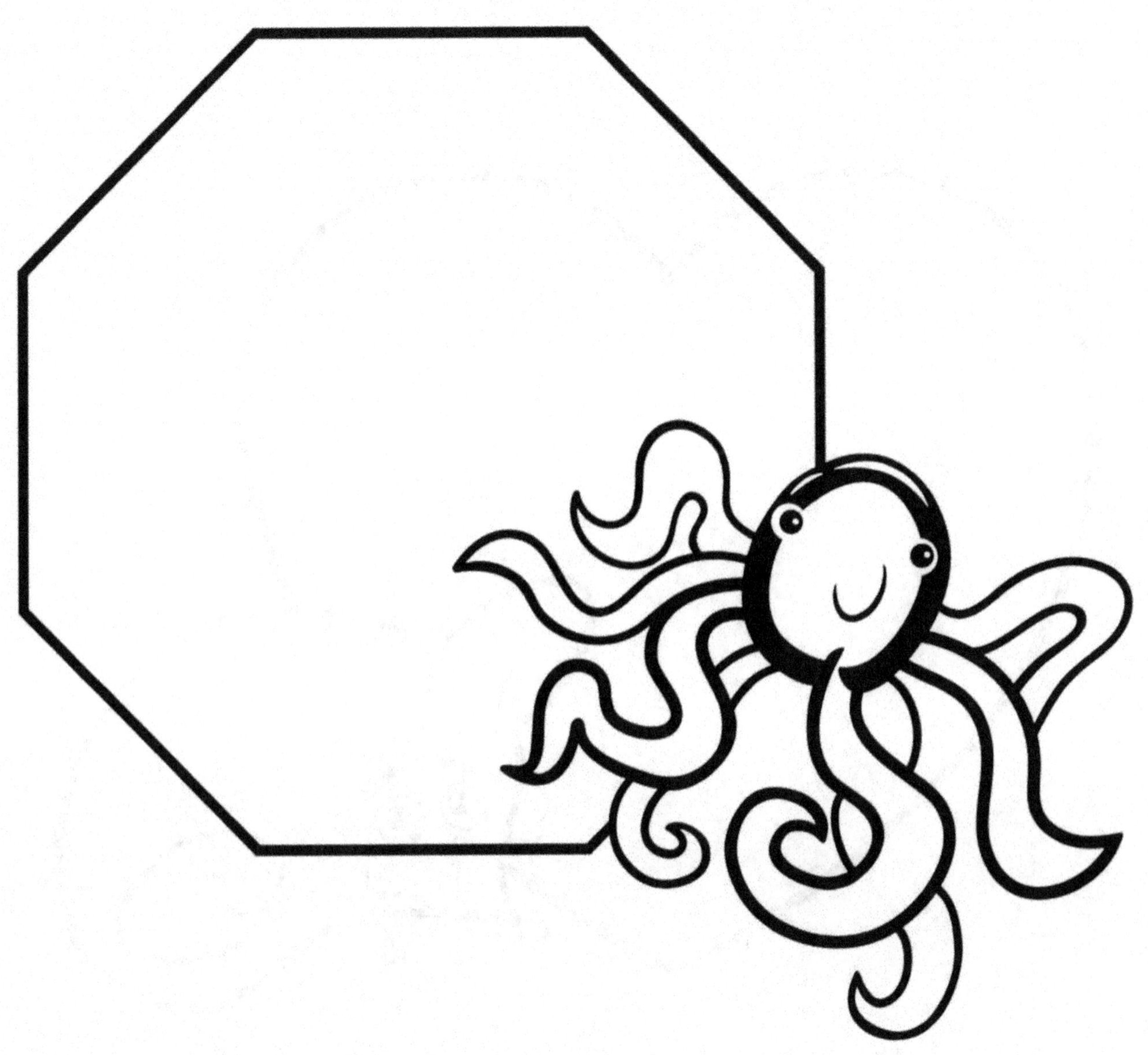

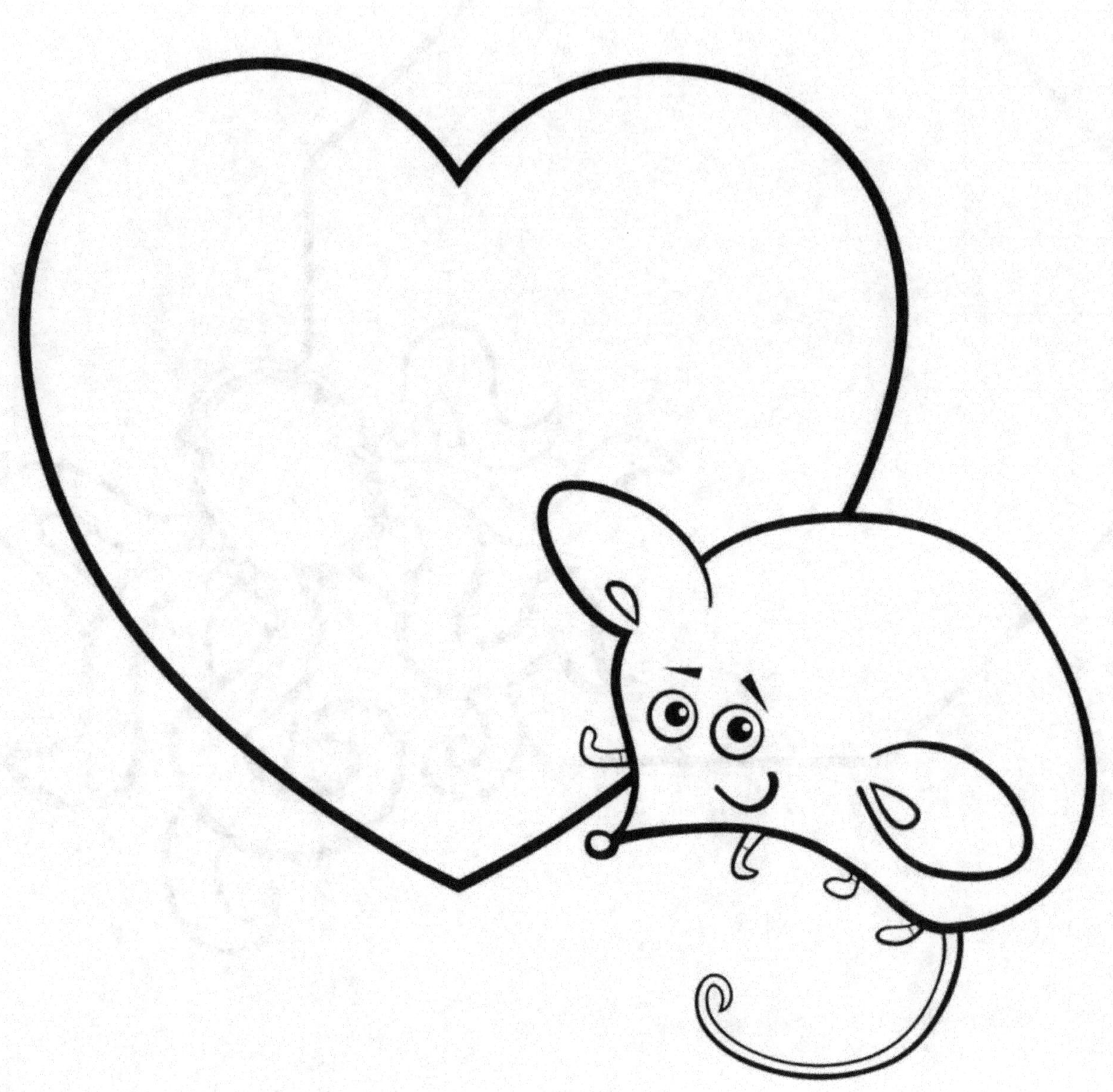

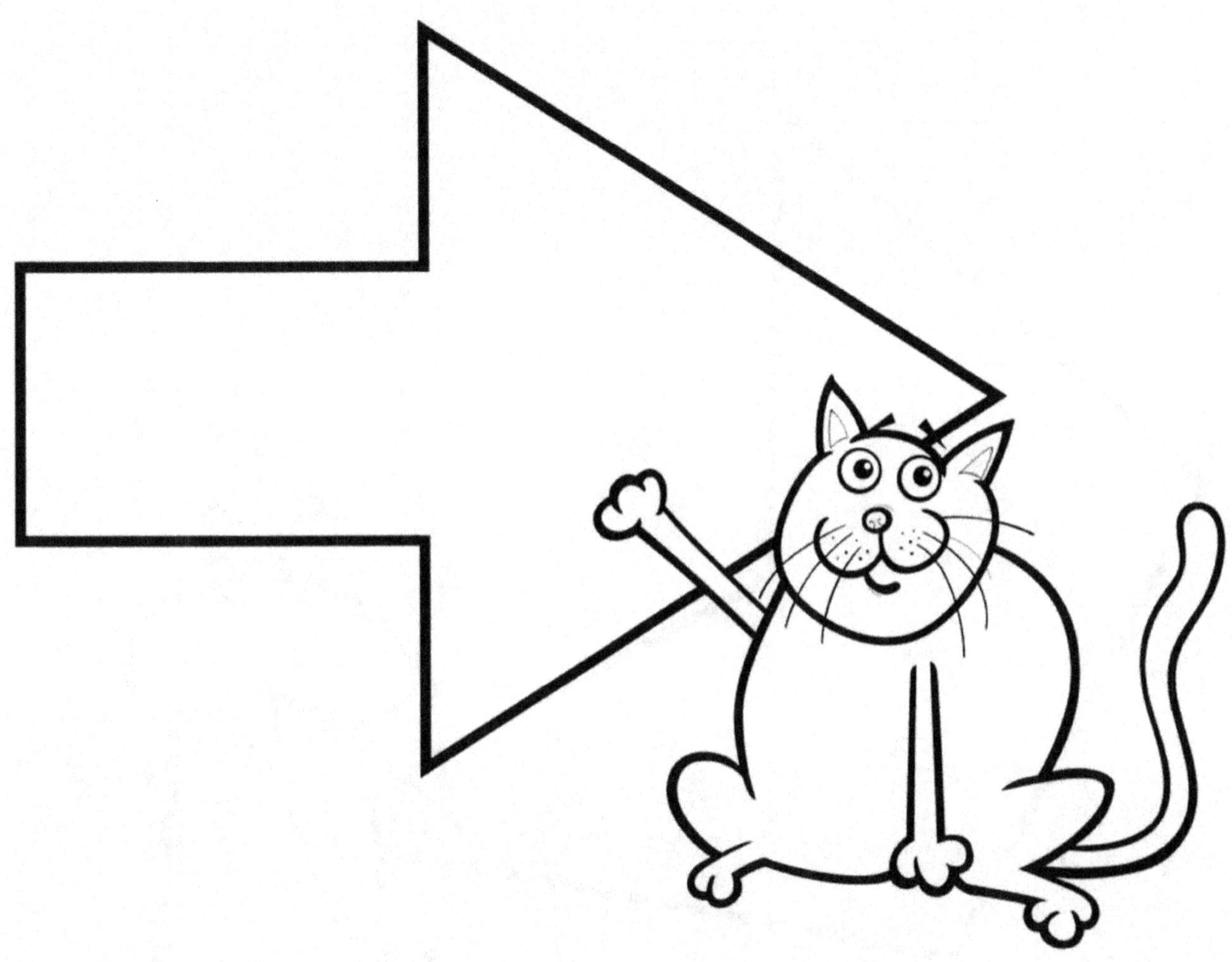

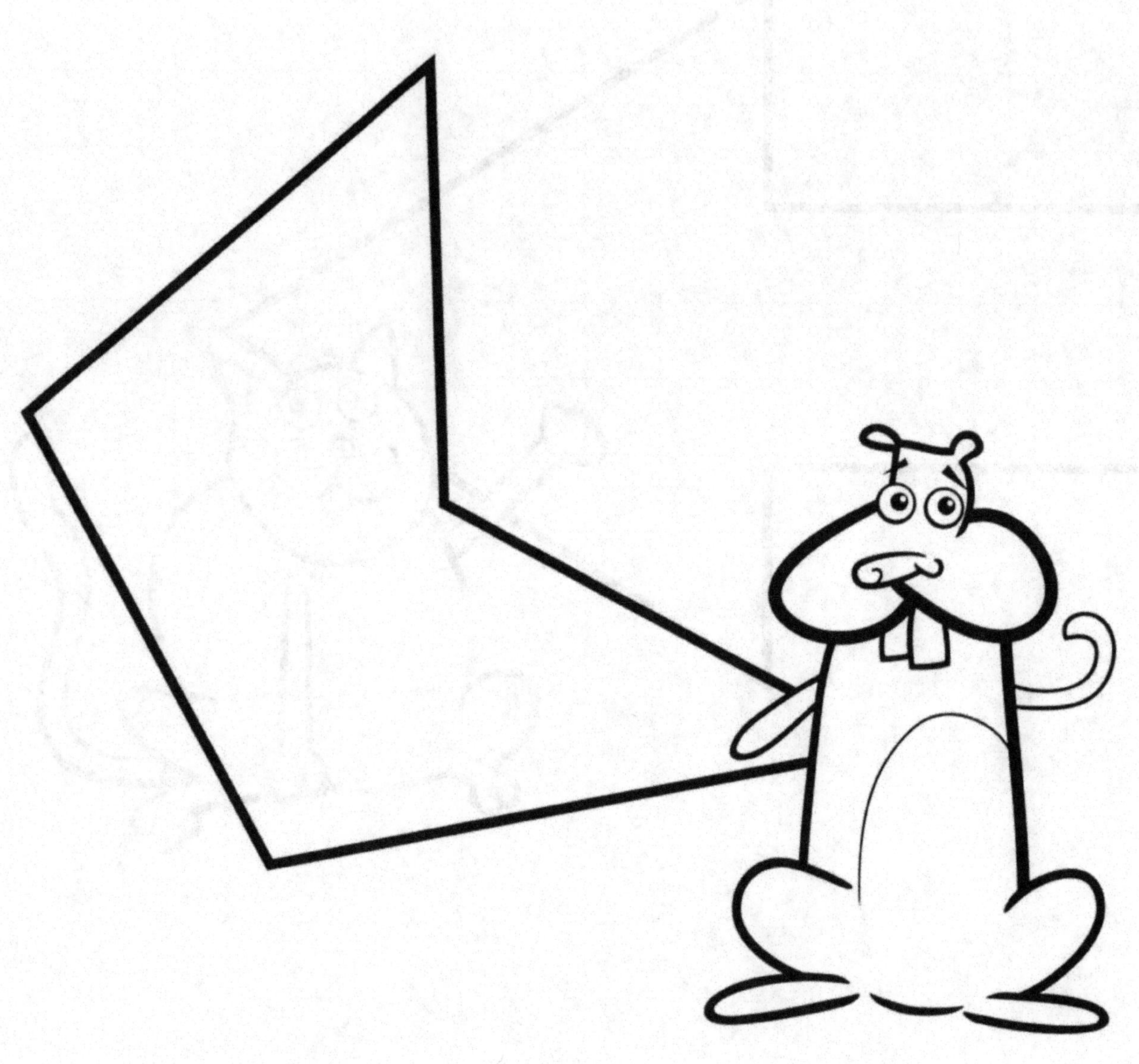

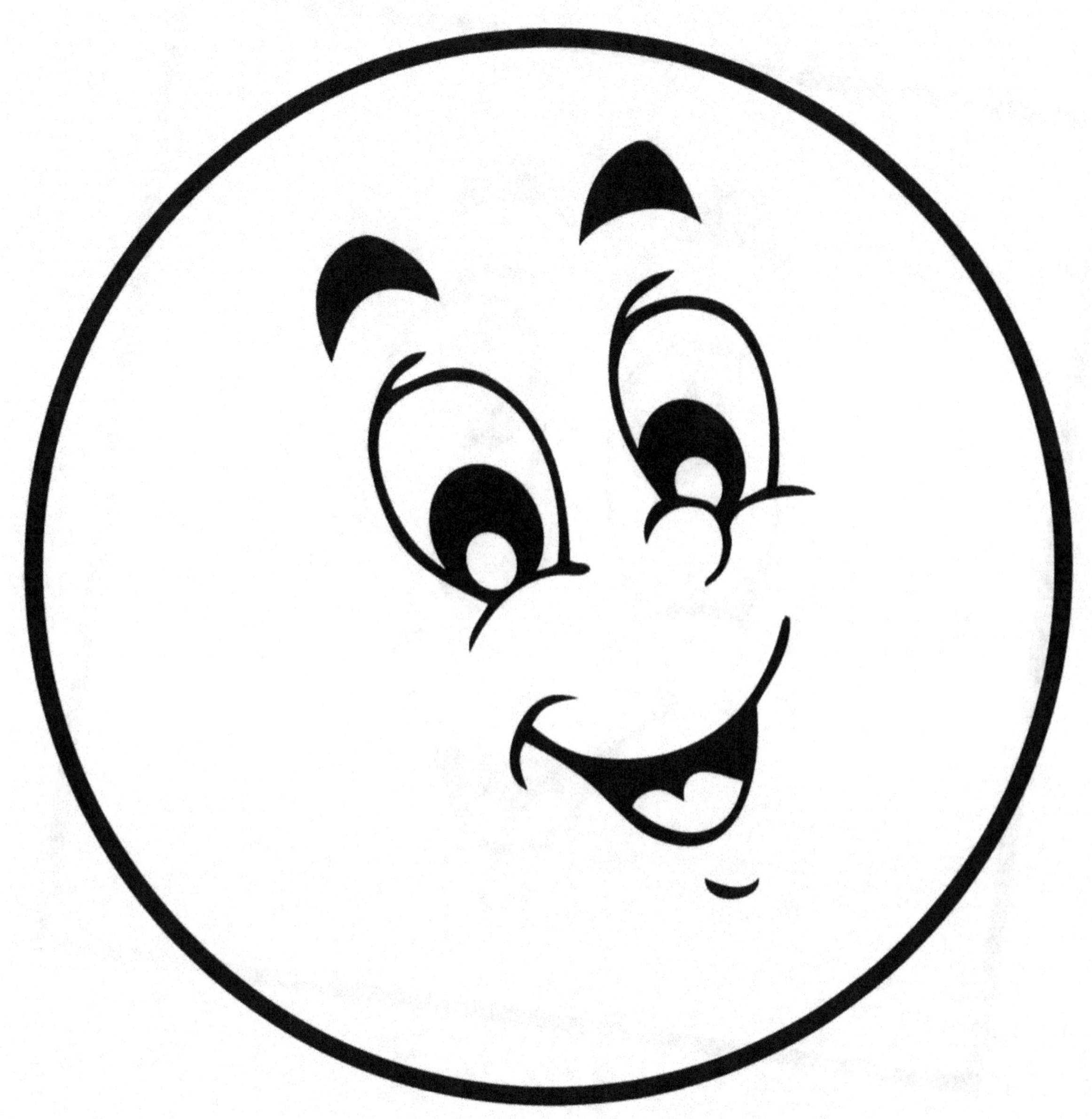

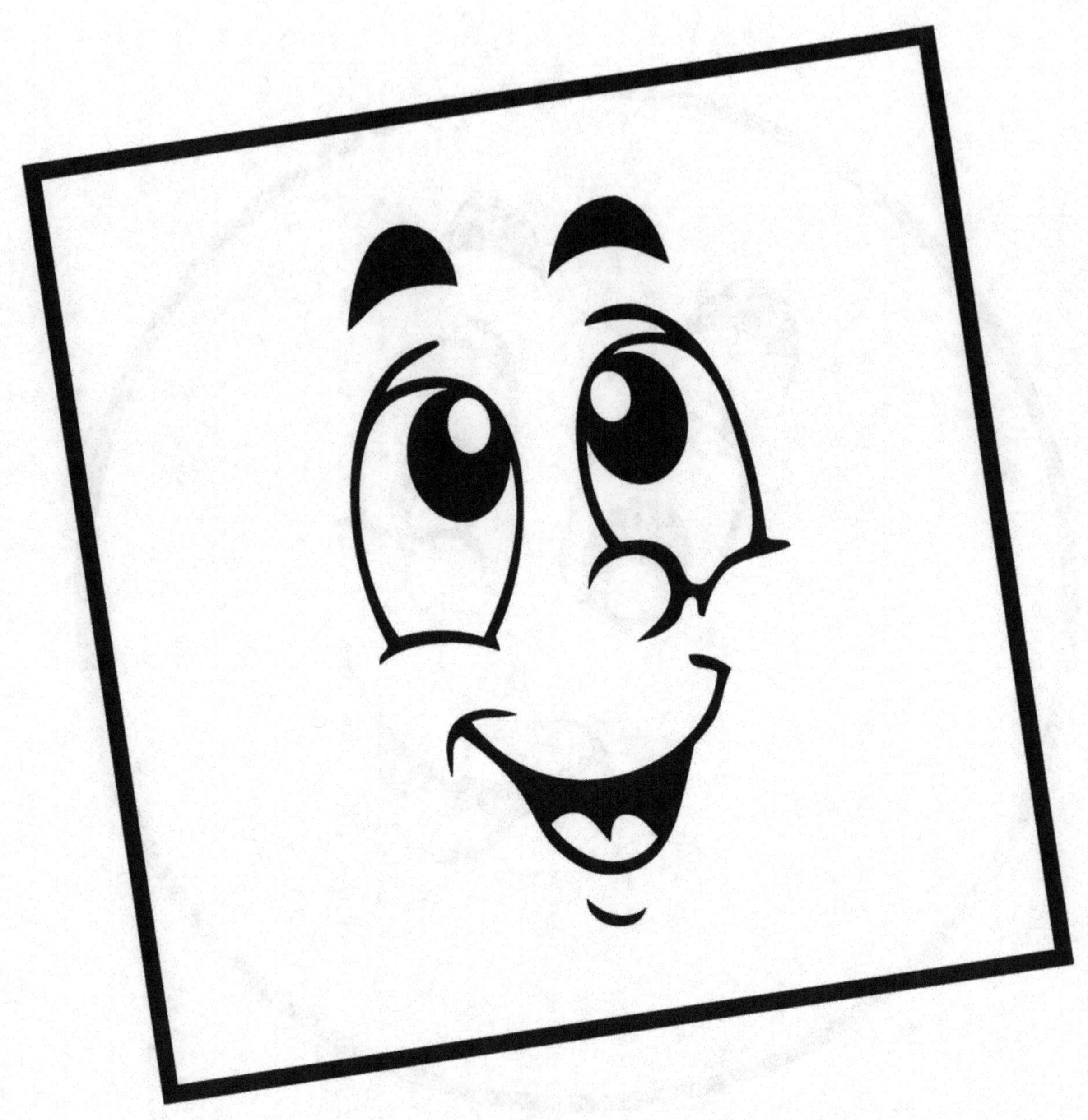

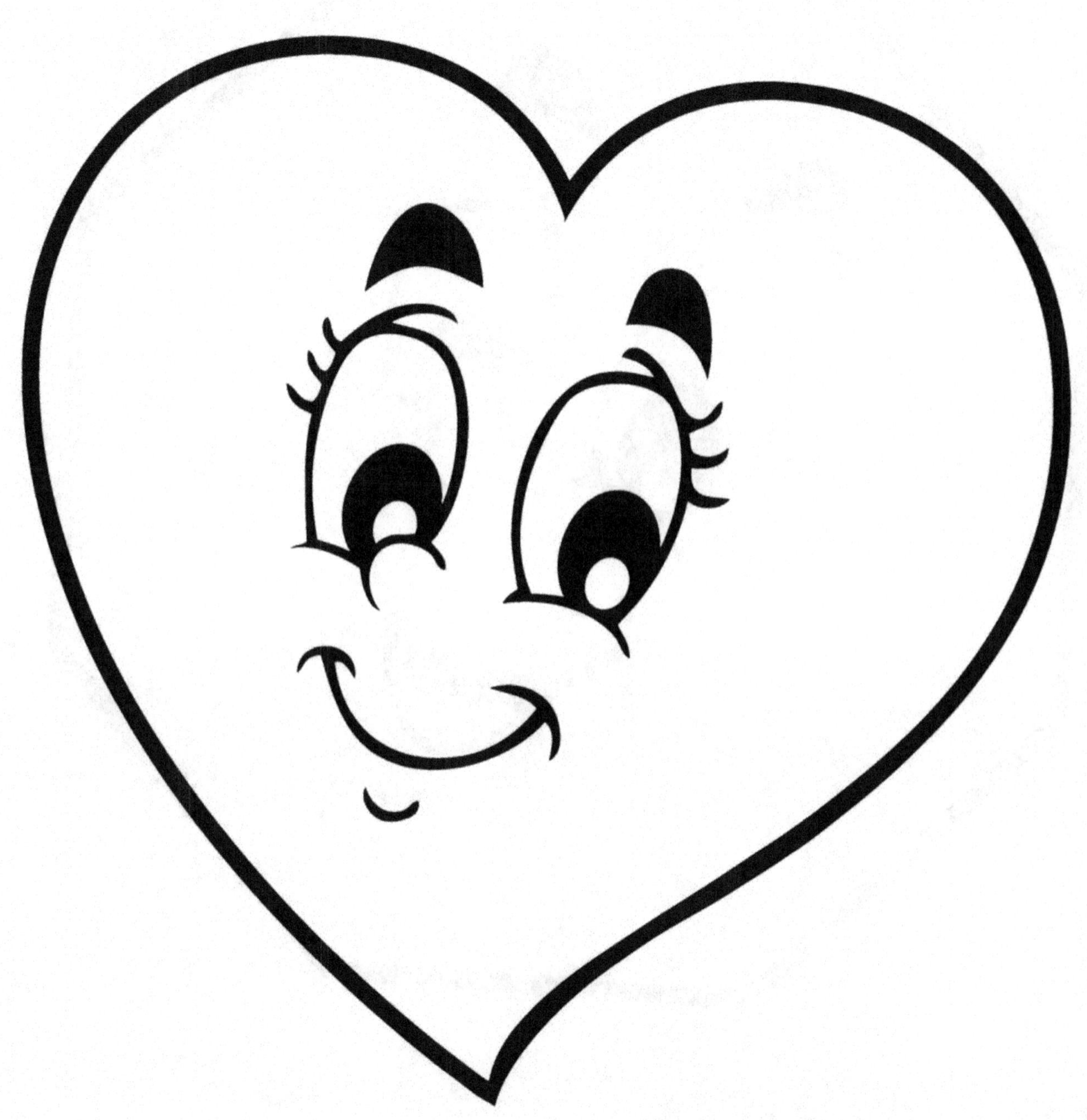

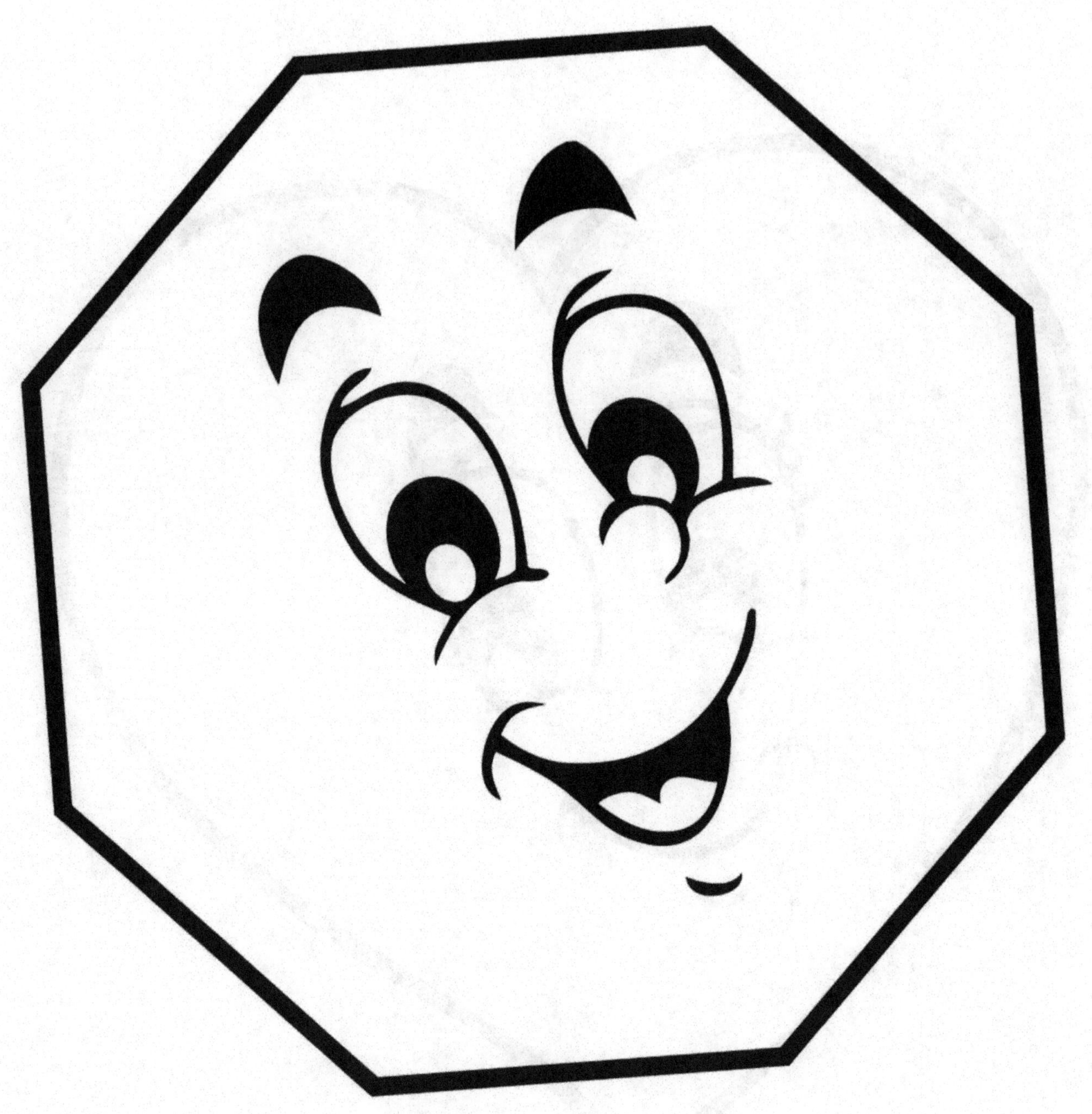

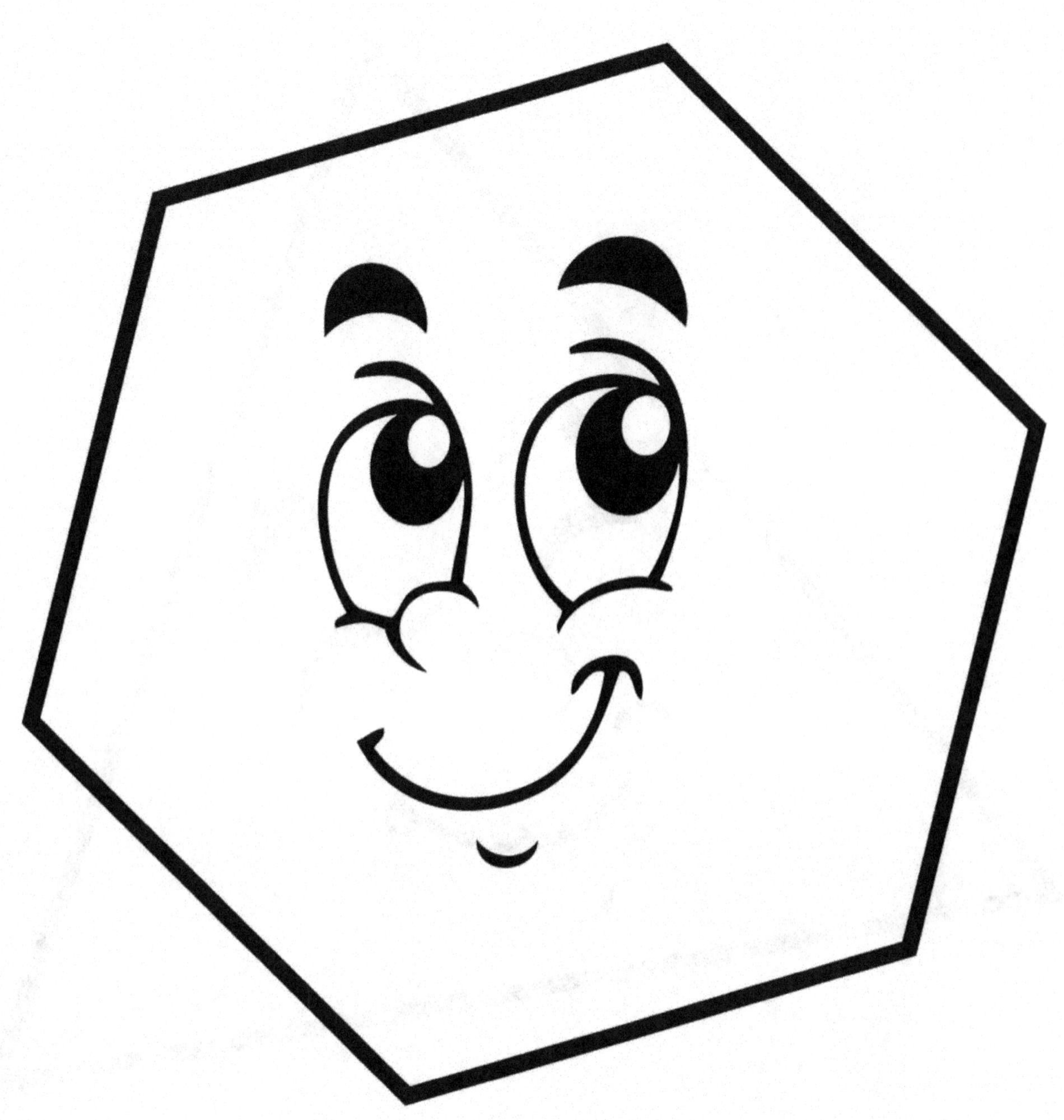

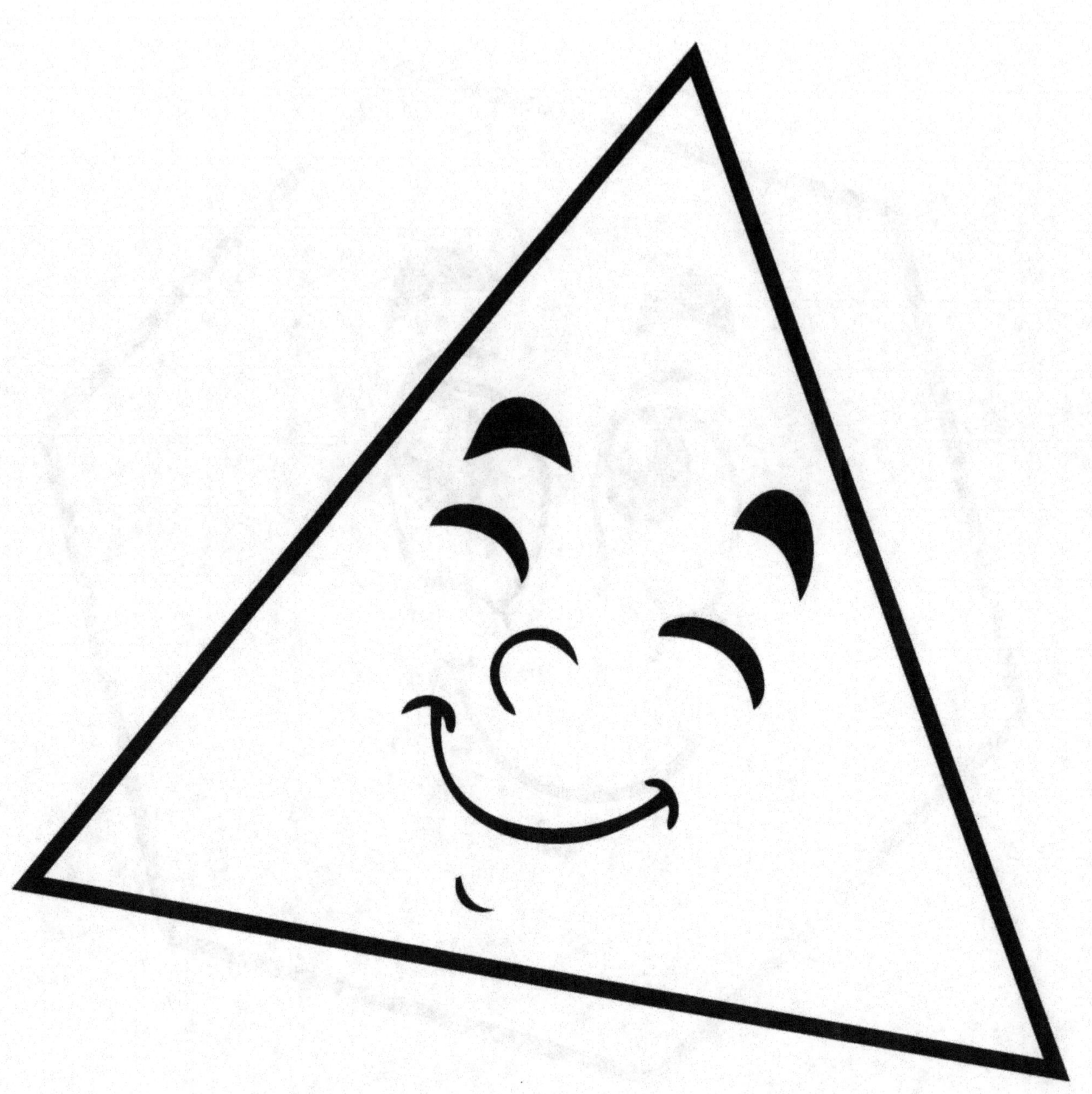

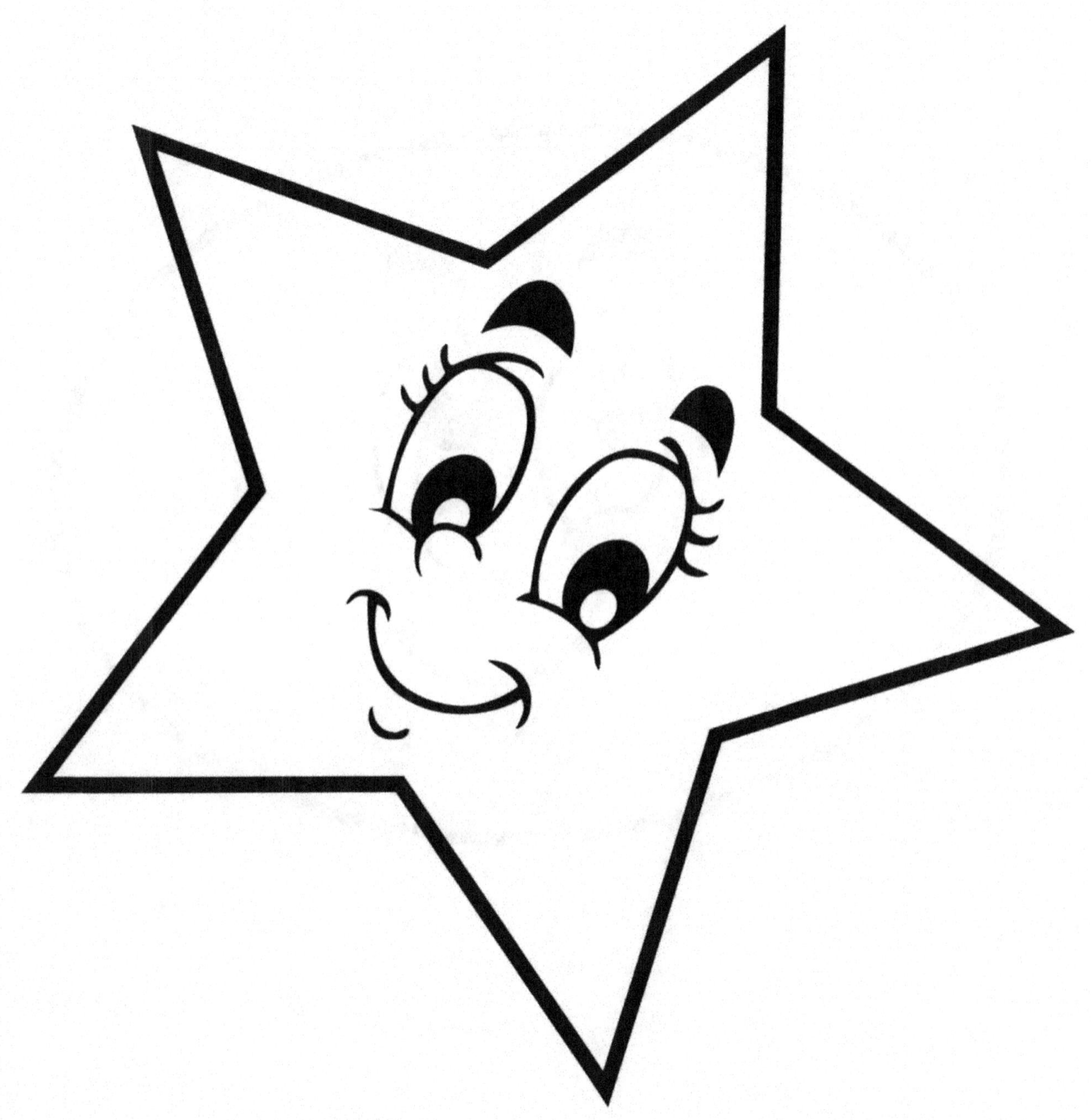

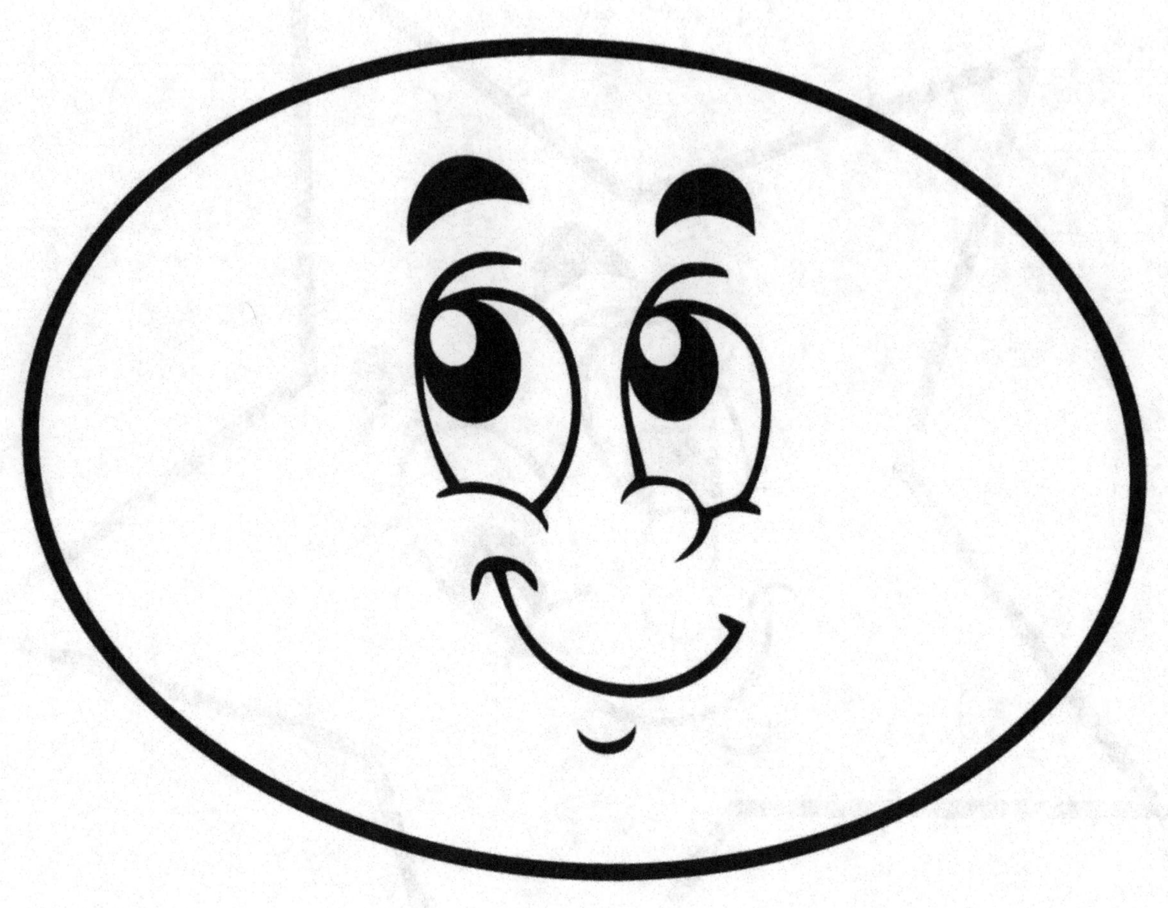

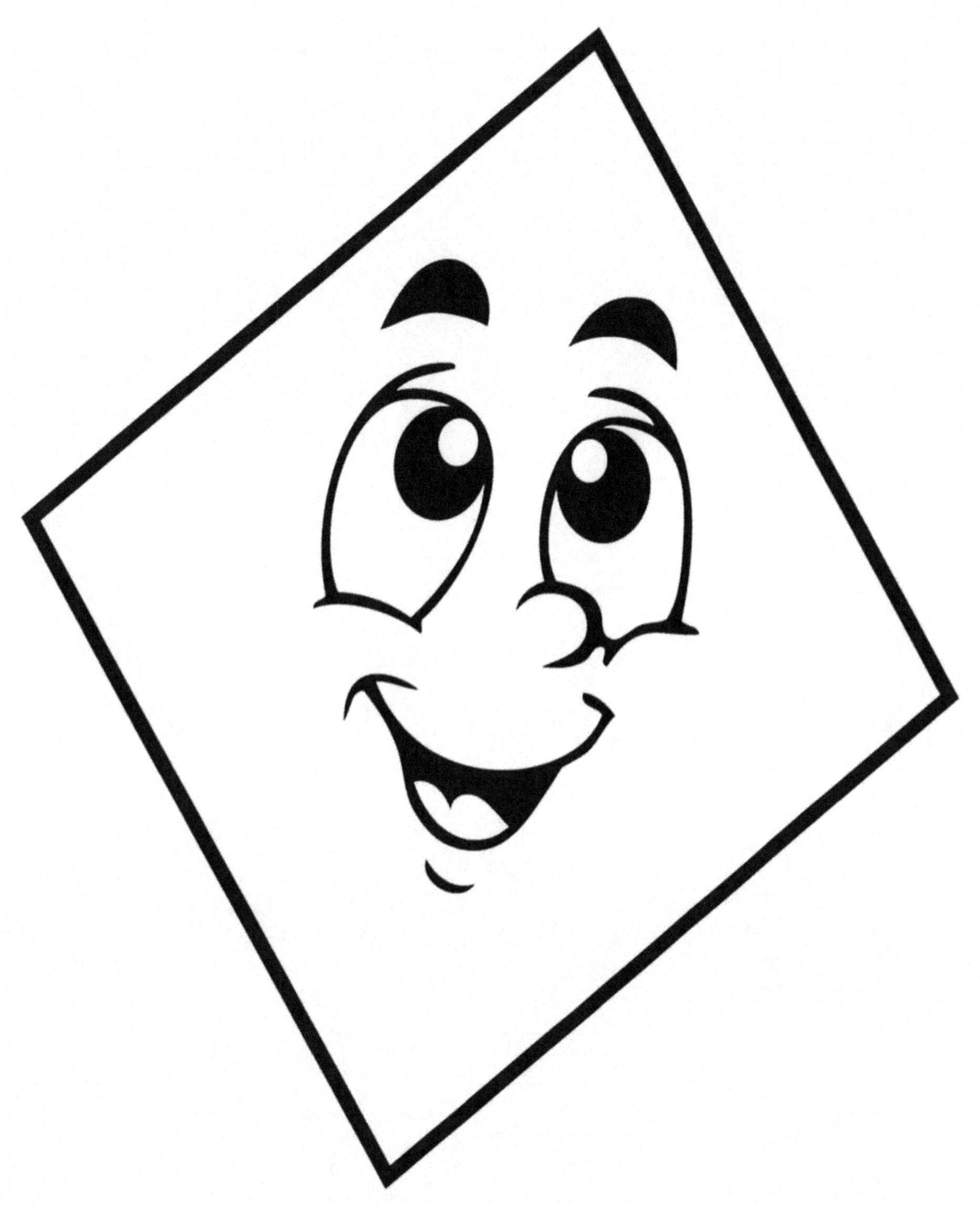

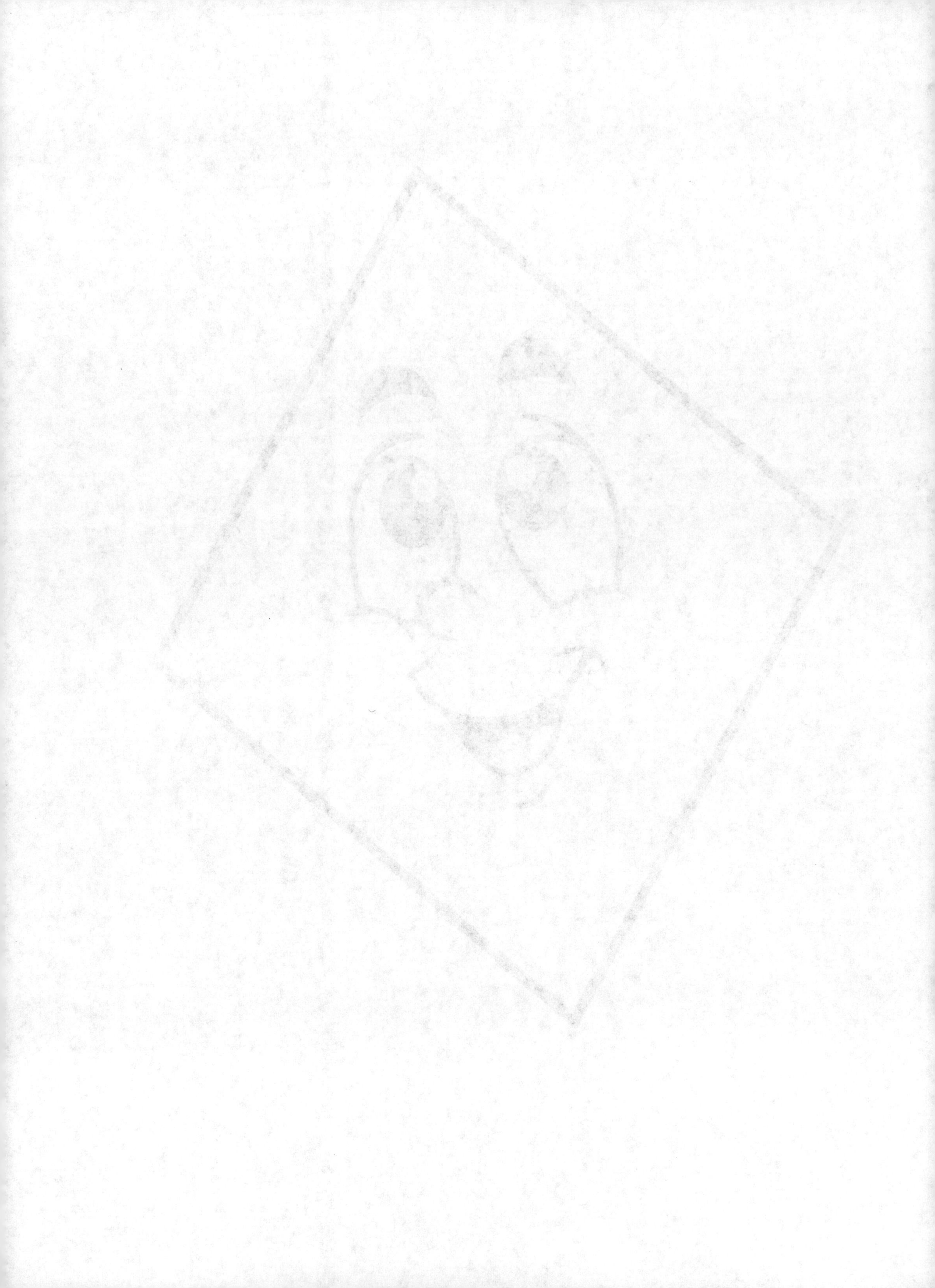